Introduction

Unleash the Power of Dragon Training:

Dragons have long captivated humanity's imagination with their majestic majesty, powerful strength, and mysterious charm. From ancient myths and legends to modern fantasy stories, these gorgeous animals have captivated people of all ages and cultures. But for those daring enough to delve into the realm of dragon training, the link formed between human and dragon goes beyond mere intrigue and becomes a partnership based on trust, respect, and mutual understanding.

In this detailed guide, we will go on a trip to discover the secrets of dragon training. Whether you're a seasoned veteran or a newcomer, this book provides vital ideas, tactics, and wisdom to help you navigate the exciting but tough world of dragon friendship. To train a dragon, specialized equipment and instruments must be used to improve communication, encourage desired behaviors, and protect the safety and well-being of both the trainer and the dragon. In chapter three of this book, we will look at the important items you'll need to properly train your dragon friend.

But why train dragons, you ask? Beyond the joy of taming a mythical monster, dragon training has significant benefits for both the trainer and the dragon. For the trainer, it provides an opportunity to tap into these gorgeous beasts' immense potential, whether for airborne transportation, labor help, or even defense against threats. Training gives the dragon a sense of purpose, belonging, and fulfillment, allowing them to release their natural skills in service of a great cause.

Throughout these pages, we'll look at the fundamentals of dragon behavior, the art of trust and bonding, necessary training commands, advanced tactics for honing particular talents, and strategies for overcoming common problems. Drawing on ancient wisdom, modern research, and personal anecdotes, we'll provide you with the knowledge and resources you need to embark on your own dragon-training adventure with confidence and conviction.

So, whether you want to soar through the sky on the back of a great dragon, defend your kingdom from marauding foes, or simply form an unbreakable friendship with a creature of legend, join us as we reveal the secrets of dragon training. Let us begin on this adventure together, into the land of fire and flying!

Chapter One

What is Dragon Training?

Dragon training is both an ancient art and a modern discipline, containing a diverse set of skills, techniques, and information aimed at developing a harmonious relationship between humans and dragons. At its foundation, dragon training is about creating mutual trust, understanding, and communication between trainer and dragon, allowing them to collaborate peacefully toward shared goals.

Dragon training has a long history, including tales, traditions, and folklore from various civilizations throughout the world. Dragons were adored as strong and magical beings by ancient humans, who frequently depicted them as symbols of wisdom, strength, and protection. As civilizations advanced, so did the interaction between humans and dragons, resulting in the creation of codified training procedures and practices.

Dragon training has grown from a mysterious and superstitious practice to a methodical and regulated discipline today. Trainers have developed more successful and humane training approaches as their understanding of dragon behavior, psychology, and physiology has advanced. Today, dragon training includes a wide range of skills, from basic obedience orders to complex aerial maneuvers and battle tactics.

Dragon training aims to create a mutually beneficial cooperation between humans and dragons. Humans can use trained dragons for a variety of purposes, including transportation, labor aid, search and rescue missions, and even battle support. Training gives dragons with mental stimulation, physical activity, as well as a sense of purpose and affiliation to human society.

Dragon training involves three essential principles that influence trainer-dragon interactions:
- Trust: Establishing trust is critical for forming a strong link between humans and dragons. Trust is built via persistent, patient, and courteous interactions.
- Communication: Clear communication is

essential for transmitting commands, expectations, and intentions between trainer and dragon. Although dragons cannot speak human languages, they can grasp gestures, voice cues, and body language.

- Positive Reinforcement: Positive reinforcement, which includes praise, prizes, and goodies, is the foundation of effective training. By rewarding desired behaviors, trainers can encourage dragons to repeat them in the future.

- Patience and Persistence: Dragon training demands patience because improvement can be sluggish and gradual. Trainers must be tenacious in their efforts, committed to the long-term success of their training programs.

In the following chapters, we'll go over these ideas in greater depth, delving into the complexities of dragon behavior, the art of creating trust and rapport, and ways for teaching dragons key commands and skills. Through devotion, perseverance, and a thorough understanding of dragon psychology, prospective trainers can unleash their dragon partners' full potential and go on an adventure, discovery, and camaraderie unlike any other.

History of Dragons and Humans

Dragons have always fascinated the human imagination, appearing in myths, tales, and cultural traditions throughout continents and civilizations. Dragons, from the majestic serpentine dragons of East Asian folklore to the fire-breathing animals of European legend, have played an important role in human storytelling throughout history.

Dragons have been depicted as powerful and supernatural beings in ancient mythology. In Mesopotamian mythology, dragons like Tiamat, the primeval goddess of chaos, represented the forces of creation and destruction. Similarly, dragons were adored in Chinese mythology as emblems of wisdom, strength, and good fortune, and were frequently portrayed as beneficent guardians of the sky and Earth.

In Western tradition, dragons were typically portrayed as villains that terrorized communities, hoarded wealth, and fought brave knights in epic stories of heroism and adventure. From the fire-breathing dragons of Greek mythology, such as the Hydra and the Chimera, to the mythical dragons slain by heroes like St. George and Beowulf, these beasts represented humanity's basic fears and hopes.

Dragons have cultural significance as symbols of strength, wisdom, protection, and transformation. Dragons were adored as divine entities in some cultures, but feared as malicious monsters to be destroyed in others. Nonetheless, the fascination with dragons has persisted, generating awe, wonder, and veneration in humans throughout history.

The interaction between dragons and humans has been complex, ranging from reverence and worship to dread and animosity. Dragons were revered as celestial beings deserving of adoration and sacrifice in some societies, but feared as destroyers and chaos in others. Despite these contrasts, people have always been drawn to dragons, hoping to understand, tame, and even dominate these mysterious beasts.

The origins of dragon training can be traced back to the desire to use dragons for practical purposes as human civilizations advanced. As a result, the art of dragon training emerged, moving from old rituals and traditions to a codified discipline with its own set of skills, procedures, and practices. From the first attempts to domesticate wild dragons to the sophisticated training programs of today, the history of dragon training demonstrates humanity's persistent fascination with these fabled creatures.

The benefits of training dragons.

Training dragons is more than just a fantasy
endeavor; it provides practical benefits to both

humans and dragons alike. As we dive more into the technique of dragon training, it becomes clear that the benefits go far beyond the excitement of taming a legendary beast.

Dragons have incredible physical strength, intelligence, and natural magical talents. Humans can use dragon training for a variety of practical purposes. From airborne transportation and cargo hauling to search and rescue missions, trained dragons provide exceptional mobility and agility in navigating a variety of terrains and conditions. Furthermore, dragons' sharp senses and formidable presence make them great allies in defending against external dangers and keeping communities safe.

Training dragons encourages mutual understanding and cooperation between people and dragons. Trainers can build trust and rapport with their dragon companions by interacting patiently and respectfully, setting the groundwork for a healthy and mutually beneficial relationship. As people and dragons learn to communicate effectively, they create a shared vocabulary of gestures, voice cues, and body language, allowing for seamless coordination and collaboration on a variety of jobs and endeavors.

Dragons benefit from training for mental

stimulation, exercise, and enrichment, which improves their general health. Dragons, like humans, are intelligent, curious, and seek purposeful activities. Dragons use training exercises to engage their minds and bodies, improving their cognitive powers and acquiring new skills and habits. Furthermore, the link formed between trainer and dragon provides emotional fulfillment and companionship to both parties, improving their lives in profound and important ways.

Training helps dragons to reach their full potential and thrive in human civilization. Trainers help dragons channel their energy and powers into useful endeavors by offering structure, instruction, and positive reinforcement. Whether they learn to perform complicated aerial acrobatics, acquire specialized talents like fire-breathing or camouflage, or hone their instincts for hunting and tracking, trained dragons become important assets to their human companions, contributing to society's greater benefit.

Dragon training promotes a culture of respect, sensitivity, and conservation for these majestic creatures. Recognizing dragons as sentient beings with their own needs, desires, and rights helps people understand the interconnection of all living things and the need of protecting biodiversity and natural ecosystems. Trained dragons act as ambassadors for their species, promoting greater understanding and compassion between people and dragons while also encouraging initiatives to safeguard and restore their ecosystems.

Dragon training aims to foster interspecies ties and bridge the gap between humans and dragons. Trainers and dragons bond deeply over shared experiences, achievements, and challenges, transcending language, culture, and species borders. In the process, they redefine the notion of friendship and camaraderie, revealing that real cooperation knows no limitations and that people and dragons may perform incredible achievements beyond imagination.

Finally, the advantages of training dragons go far beyond fiction, including practical rewards, emotional fulfillment, and spiritual development for both people and dragons. As we embark on the path of dragon training, let us use the opportunity it provides to build understanding, collaboration, and harmony between our two species, resulting in a brighter and more harmonious future for everyone.

Chapter TWO
Understanding Dragon Behavior:

Dragons, with their majestic and enigmatic presence, exhibit a diverse set of behaviors formed by millennia of evolution and adaptation. In this chapter, we will delve into the complexities of dragon behavior, examining the physiological, psychological, and social characteristics that define these amazing creatures.

Dragon species vary greatly, with each having distinct qualities and behaviors. From the strong and formidable fire dragons to the elusive and enigmatic ice dragons, the world of dragons is rich in variation. Understanding the unique characteristics and behaviors of various dragon species is critical for effective training and communication.

Dragons rely on instincts and survival strategies. Dragons, like their fabled counterparts in nature, have sharp senses, acute awareness of their environment, and tremendous defensive powers. Dragons have evolved a suite of adaptations to live in varied environments and climates, including razor-sharp claws and teeth, thick scales, and powerful wings. Understanding these natural actions is critical to developing confidence and connection with dragons.

Dragons have highly evolved social structures and communication methods within their species, while not communicating in the same way as humans. Dragons communicate their intents and form hierarchies among their groups by a range of signals, including elaborate displays of dominance and submission, vocalizations, body language, and scent marking. Trainers must learn to interpret these indications and respond correctly in order to gain the respect and cooperation of their dragon companions.

Dragons, like other animals, are territorial and fiercely protect their territories against invaders and competition. Understanding the boundaries of a dragon's domain is critical for trainers to avoid conflict and protect both themselves and their dragons. Trainers can create a harmonious relationship with their dragon companions by respecting territorial limits and creating clear communication routes.

Dragons are often depicted as solitary creatures in mythology and folklore, yet they actually exhibit complicated reproductive patterns and family dynamics in the wild. The complicated ballet of dragon reproduction includes mating rituals, wooing displays, and nest construction. Once their kids are born, dragons show tremendous parental care and devotion, raising them and teaching them critical survival skills. Understanding reproductive and family dynamics is critical for trainers dealing with breeding-age dragons.

Dragons are very adaptable and capable of learning, despite their intimidating look and old ancestry. Dragons, via observation, experimentation, and reinforcement, may learn to navigate complicated social dynamics, solve issues, and learn new abilities and behaviors. Trainers must capitalize on dragons' adaptability and create a pleasant learning environment that pushes them to reach their utmost potential.

In conclusion, understanding dragon behavior is critical for effective dragon training. By delving into the complexities of dragon physiology, psychology, and social structure, trainers may foster a greater respect for these majestic beasts while also forging stronger links of trust and collaboration.

DIFFERENT TYPES OF DRAGONS AND THEIR FEATURES

Dragons, with their different species and subspecies, display a vast range of physical characteristics, behaviors, and talents. In this section, we will look at some of the most prevalent dragon types and their distinguishing qualities.

Fire dragons are well-known for their fierce nature and flaming breath. These dragons' scales often range in hue from deep red to sparkling gold, letting them to blend in with their volcanic environments. Fire dragons are well-known for their mastery of fire magic, which they utilize both defensively and offensively to destroy their enemies and defend their domain.

Ice dragons thrive at subzero conditions, unlike their fiery counterparts. These dragons are distinguished by their icy-blue scales, crystalline wings, and cold breath, which can stop even the toughest opponents in their tracks. Ice dragons have an intrinsic understanding of ice magic, which allows them to produce blizzards, summon hailstorms, and freeze vast landscapes with a single breath.

Earth dragons are strong animals with thick scales and powerful limbs. They can burrow deep into the earth and control the landscape to their advantage. These dragons are generally found in rocky, mountainous terrain, where they build large underground lairs and stockpile valuable jewels and minerals. Earth dragons have a strong affinity for earth magic, which allows them to easily control stone, soil, and metal.

Air dragons are known for their speed, agility, and dominion over the skies. These dragons' sleek, aerodynamic bodies and massive wingspans enable them to fly freely on air currents and perform amazing aerial feats. Air dragons are generally found in high-altitude environments such as mountain peaks and cloud forests, where they hunt for prey and patrol their area with unrivaled grace and precision.

Water dragons are aquatic creatures with serpentine bodies, webbed claws, and gleaming scales that resemble sunlight on a calm lake. These dragons thrive in aquatic habitats, swimming with effortless grace and commanding the power of the waters. Water dragons have a strong affinity for water magic, which allows them to easily control tides, generate storms, and influence aquatic life.

Celestial dragons possess magical powers from the stars and skies. These dragons are rarely seen in the mortal realm, preferring to live in the celestial realms, where they study the motions of the cosmos and communicate with celestial entities. Celestial dragons have an ethereal beauty and luminosity, with shimmering scales that reflect the light from faraway stars and constellations.

Shadow dragons are mysterious animals that live in ancient woodlands and ruins. These dragons are masters of stealth and illusion, blending effortlessly into their surroundings and disappearing without a trace. Shadow dragons have a talent for shadow magic, which allows them to conceal themselves in darkness, control shadows, and trap unsuspecting prey in their web of deception.

In conclusion, the world of dragons is as varied and wondrous as the imagination. Each variety of dragon brings its own set of qualities, talents, and magic to the table, creating limitless opportunities for adventure, exploration, and discovery. Whether soaring through the heavens on the back of a fire dragon, exploring the depths of the ocean with a water dragon, or uncovering the mysteries of the universe with a celestial dragon, the adventure of dragon training is bound to be exciting, dangerous, and fascinating.

Basic Instincts and Behaviors of Dragons

Dragons, being fearsome and ancient creatures, have a complex set of reflexes and behaviors that have evolved over millenniums. Understanding these core characteristics is critical for successful dragon training and forming a strong link between human and dragon.

Dragons are apex predators with sharp senses, quick reflexes, and deadly hunting instincts. Dragons have a natural ability to hunt, pursue, and ambush prey from a young age, using their razor-sharp claws, powerful jaws, and great senses to detect even the smallest movement or scent. Trainers must be aware of dragons' predatory impulses and provide adequate opportunity for them to engage in hunting and foraging activities to satisfy their natural needs.

Dragons, like other animals, are territorial and fiercely protect their territories against invaders and competition. They use scent markers, vocalizations, and elaborate displays of dominance to show their dominance and prevent prospective attackers. To avoid sparking territorial aggressiveness, trainers must respect dragon territory limits and create clear communication routes.

Dragons are frequently depicted as solitary creatures in mythology and folklore, yet they actually exhibit complex social behaviors and group dynamics in nature. Within a dragon's domain, there may be several individuals of varied ages and genders, each holding a distinct position in the social structure. Trainers must understand these social dynamics and establish themselves as the pack's alpha or leader in order to get the respect and cooperation of their dragon partners.

During the breeding season, dragons use elaborate courtship rituals, mating displays, and nest-building behaviors to attract partners and assure offspring survival. Male dragons compete furiously for female attention, engaging in aerial duels and territorial skirmishes to establish supremacy and ensure breeding rights. Trainers must be aware of these mating tendencies and take appropriate precautions to avoid confrontations and accidents during the breeding season.

Dragons are excellent parents, nurturing and teaching their offspring survival skills. Female dragons ferociously defend their nests, whilst male dragons provide food and security for their mates and children. Trainers must respect the relationships between parents and offspring and avoid interfering with the natural upbringing process to ensure the health and well-being of both parents and children.

Dragons rely on flight to travel long distances, avoid predators, and hunt prey with incredible speed and agility. Dragons have powerful wings, lightweight bones, and aerodynamic bodies that allow them to soar through the skies and perform incredible aerial maneuvers. Trainers must provide plenty of opportunity for dragons to practice flying and perfect their aerial talents in order to keep them healthy, agile, and proficient in flight.

successful dragon training requires a grasp of dragons' basic instincts and actions. Recognizing and respecting these majestic creatures' innate characteristics allows trainers to create trust, foster collaboration, and form a deep link with their dragon companions, laying the groundwork for a gratifying and successful partnership founded on mutual respect and understanding.

How Dragons Communicate

Communication is important to any successful connection, including the tie between people and dragons. Dragons may not interact in the same manner that people do, but they do have highly evolved forms of communication that are necessary for navigating their complicated social dynamics and collaborating with their human counterparts.

Dragons employ various vocalizations to communicate, express emotions, and build social hierarchies in their populations. These vocalizations range from deep, rumbling growls and roars to high-pitched screeches and chirps, and each has a distinct function in dragon communication. Trainers must learn to decipher these vocalizations and respond appropriately in order to comprehend their dragon partners' wants and intentions.

Dragon communication relies heavily on body language, which includes posture, gestures, and facial expressions to transmit nuanced signals. Dragons utilize body language to convey dominance, submission, aggression, and affection, which can reveal important information about their attitude and mindset. Trainers must closely monitor their dragon companions and learn to decipher their body language in order to establish rapport and trust.

Dragons communicate by gestures and postures, as well as vocalizations and body language, with their human trainers. These motions may involve raising or lowering their wings, puffing out their chest, or tilting their head to one side, all of which indicate a specific message or intention. Trainers must be aware of these subtle signs and respond correctly to ensure clear and successful communication with their dragon companions.

Dragons may be able to connect telepathically with humans, allowing for direct exchange of thoughts, emotions, and intentions across linguistic limitations. This telepathic relationship is frequently formed via great trust and mutual understanding between humans and dragons, allowing them to converse fluidly and coordinate their activities with pinpoint accuracy and efficiency.

Dragons use intrinsic magical talents to communicate, including breath weapons, elemental magic, and telekinetic gestures. These magical signals may send complicated messages and directives to both dragons and humans, making them an effective means of communication in situations where vocalizations or body language are insufficient.

Dragons use environmental cues to communicate

and navigate their surroundings. These cues may include scent markings, territorial boundaries, and landmarks that act as communication and navigation points. Trainers must be aware of these environmental cues and use them to improve communication and cooperation with their dragons.

in summary, Dragons communicate via a variety of means, including vocalizations, body language, gestures, telepathy, magical signals, and environmental clues, to convey information, express emotions, and coordinate their movements. Understanding and appreciating these communication strategies enables trainers to develop clear and effective channels of communication with their dragon partners, creating trust, cooperation, and mutual understanding.

CHAPTER THREE
preparing for Dragon Training:

Before commencing on the thrilling voyage of dragon training, it is critical to establish a firm foundation of knowledge, skills, and resources to ensure the success and safety of both trainer and dragon. In this chapter, we'll look at the important stages and preparations needed to embark on the journey of a lifetime: training your dragon.

To prepare for dragon training, it's important to first learn about their physiology, anatomy, and biology. This knowledge will provide vital insights into dragons' specific wants and requirements, allowing trainers to provide appropriate care, nourishment, and medical attention. Trainers should get familiar with the exact qualities and traits of the dragon species they plan to train, as each species may have different nutritional preferences, habitat requirements, and behavioral inclinations.

Building trust and connection between trainer and dragon is crucial for successful training. Building trust takes time, patience, and consistency, as dragons are inherently cautious and apprehensive of new humans. Trainers should treat their dragon companions with respect, empathy, and understanding, gradually building trust via good interactions, rewards, and reinforcement. Trainers can form a strong connection with their dragons based on mutual respect and cooperation by laying a firm foundation of trust and rapport.

Creating a Safe and Stimulating Environment: Dragons flourish in surroundings that offer mental stimulation, physical activity, and social interactions. Trainers should provide a safe and engaging environment for their dragons, including enrichment activities, training equipment, and socialization chances. Dragons' health and well-being depend on access to natural factors such as sunlight, fresh air, and wide spaces, since they require regular exercise and mental stimulation to thrive.

To effectively teach dragons, customized approaches and plans must be developed based on their unique demands and skills. Trainers should get familiar with tried-and-true training approaches including positive reinforcement, shaping, and desensitization, which emphasize clear communication, consistency, and patience. Trainers can use these strategies to encourage desired behaviors, discourage bad habits, and strengthen the link between humans and dragons.

To successfully train dragons, trainers must collect sufficient materials and equipment. This could include teaching tools like clickers, target sticks, and harnesses, as well as protection equipment like gloves, helmets, and body armor for properly handling and dealing with dragons. Trainers should also ensure that their dragon partners have access to excellent food, water, housing, and veterinary care in order to meet their basic needs and maintain their health and well-being.

Creating a training plan and schedule is crucial for consistent, structured, and effective dragon training. Trainers should set specific goals, targets, and milestones for their training program, breaking down complex behaviors into small steps and gradually increasing the challenge as their dragon companions develop.

Establishing and keeping to a regular training program will assist reinforce desired behaviors and build momentum toward meeting training objectives.

Trainers should seek support and guidance from seasoned specialists, mentors, and fellow trainers who specialize in dragon training. Joining dragon training communities, whether local or online, can provide useful resources, guidance, and support to new trainers. Trainers can overcome obstacles, celebrate victories, and advance as practitioners of the noble art of dragon training by sharing their experiences, exchanging ideas, and learning from one another.

preparing for dragon training takes meticulous planning, preparation, and dedication to ensure the success and safety of both the trainer and the dragon. Understanding dragon physiology, developing trust and rapport, creating a safe and stimulating environment, developing training techniques and strategies, securing necessary resources and equipment, developing a training plan and schedule, and seeking support and guidance from experienced professionals can help trainers embark on the adventure of dragon training with confidence, enthusiasm, and a sense of purpose.

Creating a Suitable Environment for Training

Creating an environment favorable to efficient dragon training is critical to the success of your efforts. Dragons, like other intelligent and sentient beings, want situations that are safe, engaging, and favorable to learning. In this section, we'll look at the key elements of establishing such an environment for your dragon friend.

To properly teach your dragon, it's important to first understand their habitat requirements. Temperature, humidity, space, and environmental enrichment requirements vary among dragon species. Researching your dragon species' natural habitat will provide significant insights into the circumstances they require to thrive, which you can then duplicate in your training setting.

Providing adequate space and freedom of mobility is crucial for dragons, since they need to stretch, exercise, and explore their surroundings. When building your training setting, make sure it leaves enough area for your dragon to travel freely without feeling constrained or restricted. Indoor rooms should be large and well-ventilated, and outdoor places should be safe and devoid of potential risks.

Creating enrichment opportunities is crucial for keeping dragons engaged during training sessions. Include a range of enrichment activities in your training environment, such as puzzle toys, climbing structures, and foraging opportunities, to keep your dragon companion mentally stimulated and avoid boredom. Rotating enrichment materials on a regular basis will keep your dragon interested and curious, encouraging them to explore and develop new talents.

Prioritize safety and security when teaching your dragon companion. To avoid accidents or injuries, remove any potential hazards or harmful materials from the training environment, including sharp edges, toxic plants, and electrical wires. Secure outdoor training facilities with strong fence or barriers to prevent escape and keep out undesirable intruders or predators.

Dragons benefit from exposure to natural factors, including sunlight, fresh air, and natural substrates. Whenever possible, combine these components into your training environment to improve your dragon's health and well-being. Outdoor training sessions in a secure, fenced-in location allow your dragon to drink up the sun, breathe fresh air, and dig in the mud, all of which provide vital sensory and brain stimulation.

Establishing Comfortable Resting locations: Dragons require locations to relax and recharge in between training sessions. Provide comfortable nesting materials, such as soft bedding or hay, in a quiet, covered part of the training area where your dragon can rest and relax. Access to fresh water and good food is also critical for keeping your dragon healthy and vital during training.

To foster a pleasant learning environment for your dragon, prioritize creating a safe, cherished, and respected space. Positive reinforcement strategies, such as praise, food, and prizes, can help your dragon partner develop desirable habits and confidence. Be patient, consistent, and empathic in your interactions with your dragon, and acknowledge their development and accomplishments along the way.

Creating an appropriate environment for dragon training necessitates careful consideration of your dragon's habitat demands, safety concerns, and enrichment preferences. You may build an environment in which your dragon partner can thrive, learn, and grow to their full potential by providing adequate space, enrichment opportunities, safety precautions, access to natural elements, comfortable resting spots, and a pleasant learning atmosphere.

Essential Equipment and Tools for Dragon Training

To train a dragon, specialized equipment and instruments must be used to improve communication, encourage desired behaviors, and protect the safety and well-being of both the trainer and the dragon. In this section, we will look at the important items you'll need to properly train your dragon friend.

Using **PROTECTIVE GEAR** is crucial when handling dragons, especially if they are young or tame. Gloves, arm guards, and body protection are crucial for protecting oneself against scratches, bites, and other potential injuries during training sessions. Choose sturdy protective gear that provides flexibility and protection while allowing you to move freely.

A properly fitted **HARNESS AND LEASH** are essential for managing and directing your dragon during training sessions. Choose a harness developed exclusively for dragons that distributes pressure uniformly over their body and eliminates chafing and discomfort. Attach a durable leash to the harness to keep your dragon under control and prevent it from wandering off or getting into danger during training activities.

A **TRAINING CLICKER** is a small handheld gadget that makes a distinctive clicking sound when pressed. Clickers are used to signal to your dragon that they have correctly done a desired behavior, allowing for exact scheduling and reinforcement during training sessions. Clickers are a useful and versatile tool for molding behaviors, documenting successes, and promoting clear communication between trainer and dragon.

A **TARGET STICK** guides and shapes your dragon's movements during training activities. It is made up of a long, lightweight stick with a colored or textured tip that your dragon may touch or track with their nose or paw. Target sticks can help educate your dragon to target specific items or locations, shape complicated actions, and improve focus and attention during training sessions.

A **TREAT BAG** is a useful tool for transporting and giving incentives during training sessions. Select a treat bag that fits securely around your waist or belt and has many sections for holding various sorts of treats. Keep a variety of high-value treats, such as little pieces of meat or fruit, in your treat pouch to reward your dragon for good conduct and encourage them to participate enthusiastically in training sessions.

TRAINING PROPS AND EQUIPMENT: Depending on your dragon's training goals, you may require various props and equipment to facilitate workouts. This could contain agility equipment like tunnels, hurdles, and weave poles to help your dragon negotiate obstacles, as well as target objects, platforms, and perches to practice targeting, balancing, and stationing habits. Choose props and equipment that are safe, durable, and suitable for your dragon's size, age, and skill level.

To prevent accidents and injuries during training sessions, keep a well-stocked **FIRST AID BAG** on standby. Your first aid box should include basic goods like bandages, antiseptic wipes, gauze pads, adhesive tape, and scissors, as well as any specialty products advised by your veterinarian for treating dragon-specific injuries or illnesses. Familiarize yourself with the contents of your first aid bag and understand how to perform basic first aid techniques in an emergency.

Having the appropriate equipment and instruments is critical for successful dragon training. By purchasing protective gear, a harness and leash, a training clicker, a target stick, a reward pouch, training props and equipment, and a first aid kit, you can establish a safe, successful, and pleasurable training environment for you and your dragon companion. With the right tools and tactics at your disposal, you'll be well-prepared to go on the thrilling path of training your dragon to be the best it can be.

Safety precautions

When going on a dragon training trip, it is critical to ensure the safety of both the trainer and the dragon. Dragons are fierce and unpredictable creatures, so training them takes meticulous planning, preparation, and adherence to safety standards. In this section, we'll look at important safety precautions to keep in mind throughout the course.

To train dragons effectively, it's important to first understand their behavior and body language. Recognizing signals of tension, anger, or hostility in your dragon friend can help you predict and minimize potential safety risks before they become serious. Take the time to study and learn your dragon's specific signs and signals, and always prioritize their comfort and well-being while training.

Clear communication is essential for preserving safety throughout training sessions. Establishing a consistent mode of communication between trainer and dragon, such as verbal cues, hand gestures, or clicker training, will assist to avoid misunderstandings and ensure that your dragon understands what is expected of them. Use consistent, positive reinforcement approaches to encourage desired behaviors while effectively redirecting or discouraging negative actions.

Using Protective Gear: Protective gear reduces the chance of harm during training sessions. Wear strong gloves, arm guards, and body protection to protect yourself from scratches, bites, and other potential threats. When working with larger or more powerful dragons, consider wearing a helmet or other protective headgear. To give the best protection and comfort, make sure that all protective gear is correctly fitted and maintained.

Avoiding High-Risk habits: Some habits increase the risk of harm during training sessions and should be avoided wherever possible. This could include reaching for or grasping your dragon's head or neck, attempting to restrict or overwhelm them, or indulging in rough play or physical combat. Instead, use positive reinforcement tactics to create trust and collaboration while also respecting your dragon's boundaries and limitations.

To ensure a safe and secure training environment for you and your dragon, remove potential risks such as obstructions, sharp items, and toxic substances. When performing outdoor training sessions, make sure the space is adequately gated or enclosed to prevent escape and keep out unwanted strangers or predators. To maintain safety standards, evaluate training equipment and props on a regular basis for signs of wear or damage, and replace or repair them as necessary.

Seeking Professional Guidance: If you're not sure how to safely teach your dragon or face behavior concerns, seek help from qualified trainers or animal behaviorists. They can offer useful insights, advice, and assistance to help you overcome obstacles and protect the safety and well-being of both you and your dragon partner. Remember that there is no shame in seeking assistance for your dragon's well-being.

Monitoring Health and Wellbeing:
During training sessions, keep an eye out for signs of weariness, tension, or discomfort in your

dragon. Give your dragon frequent breaks and opportunities for relaxation and hydration, and check with a veterinarian if you have any concerns about its physical or emotional health. Prioritizing your dragon's well-being and safety will guarantee that training sessions are enjoyable and beneficial for both of you.

In short, safety should always be the first consideration when training a dragon. Understanding dragon behavior, establishing clear communication, using protective gear, avoiding high-risk behaviors, providing safe training environments, seeking professional guidance when necessary, and monitoring your dragon's health and well-being can all help you create a safe and supportive training environment that fosters trust, cooperation, and mutual respect between you and your dragon companion.

CHAPTER FOUR
Establishing Trust and Bonding

Establishing a solid foundation of trust and bonding is critical for a successful and rewarding connection with your dragon partner. In this chapter, we will look at the essential principles and approaches for building trust, developing rapport, and strengthening the link between humans and dragons.

Patience and understanding are essential for gaining trust and bonding with your dragon. Understand that developing a strong relationship requires time and cannot be rushed. Be patient with your dragon as they adjust to their new surroundings and develop trust in you as their trainer and companion. Approach encounters with empathy, understanding, and compassion, taking into account your dragon's specific requirements and characteristics.

Building trust and confidence with your dragon requires consistent and reliable behavior. Be constant in your actions, words, and training methods, and keep your pledges and commitments. Create a consistent pattern for training sessions, feeding times, and everyday activities to give your dragon a sense of comfort and stability. Over time, being dependable and consistent will earn you your dragon's trust and respect.

Positive reinforcement is an effective way to create trust and reinforce desired behaviors in your dragon. Use praise, gifts, and awards to stimulate and encourage your dragon throughout training sessions, and celebrate their accomplishments along the way. Instead of penalizing or correcting unwanted behaviors, focus on rewarding the ones you want to see more of. Positive reinforcement fosters a positive link with training, strengthening your bond with your dragon.

Respect and empathy are essential for healthy relationships, including those between humans and dragons. Always treat your dragon with kindness, dignity, and respect, while also acknowledging their autonomy and individuality. Respect their boundaries and preferences, and don't force them into circumstances that make them uncomfortable or stressful. Empathy may be developed by putting yourself in the shoes of your dragon and understanding their perspective, emotions, and wants.

Spending quality time together strengthens the link between you and your dragon. Participate in activities that your dragon enjoys, such as training sessions, walks, flights, or fun, and make an effort to be present and involved throughout these interactions. Take advantage of these opportunities to learn more about your dragon's personality, preferences, and peculiarities, and enjoy the camaraderie and mutual affection that grows as you spend time together.

To maintain a happy connection with your dragon, it's important to create mutual trust. Be trustworthy and dependable in your activities, and don't violate your dragon's faith with inconsistency or broken promises. Trust your dragon to express their wants and preferences with you, and pay close attention to their cues and signals. By developing mutual trust and understanding, you will strengthen your bond with your dragon and lay the groundwork for future adventures together.

Developing trust and bonding with your dragon involves patience, persistence, and dedication. Be patient with yourself and your dragon as you work through the ups and downs of the bonding process, and don't be disheartened by failures or problems. Stay focused on developing a deep and meaningful relationship with your dragon, and celebrate any progress you achieve together, no matter how tiny.

In the end, developing trust and bonding with your dragon is a wonderful and joyful experience that necessitates patience, consistency, and empathy. You can form a deep and long-lasting friendship with your dragon partner by addressing interactions with kindness, respect, and understanding, as well as prioritizing quality time together. With time, patience, and effort, you'll form a connection that enhances both of your lives and opens up a world of limitless opportunities.

Tips for Bonding with Your Dragon

Bonding with your dragon is a deeply satisfying process that enhances your relationship and builds mutual trust and understanding. In this section, we will look at a range of strategies for strengthening your bond with your dragon friend.

Spending quality time together is an effective approach to bond with your dragon. Engage in activities that your dragon enjoys, such as training sessions, outdoor expeditions, or simply relaxing together in a comfy location. Make an effort to be present and aware at these times, and appreciate the chance to connect with your dragon on a deeper level.

Bonding with your dragon involves physical contact and affection, which can enhance your bond. Gently stroke your dragon's scales or feathers, scratch their favorite region, or give them a gentle massage to help them relax and feel safe in your company. Be aware of your dragon's body language and cues, and respect their boundaries and preferences about physical contact.

Building trust with your dragon requires clear and regular communication. To improve communication and strengthen your bond, use trust-building exercises like target training, desensitization, and cooperative activities. Use positive reinforcement tactics to encourage desirable actions and foster mutual trust and respect.

Sharing meals and snacks can strengthen the bond between you and your dragon. Offer your dragon's favorite treats as rewards during training or as a special treat for good behavior. Share meals together, either by hand-feeding your dragon or by eating in their company, and use mealtime as an occasion to bond and connect more deeply.

Exploring new areas together can enhance your friendship with your dragon. Take your dragon on trips to new locales like parks, forests, and beaches, and let them explore and interact with their surroundings. Use these opportunities to bond with your dragon and make lifelong memories together.

Interacting with your dragon through games and enrichment activities can foster a strong friendship. Toys, puzzles, and interactive activities can help your dragon's cognitive and physical exercise. Include playtime in your everyday routine and make it a consistent component of your bonding experience with your dragon.

Consistency and reliability are essential for creating trust and strengthening your friendship with your dragon. Be constant in your actions, words, and training methods, and keep your pledges and commitments. Create a consistent pattern for training sessions, feeding times, and everyday activities to give your dragon a sense of comfort and stability.

Building trust and establishing your friendship with your dragon requires active listening and reacting to their needs. Pay attention to your dragon's body language, vocalizations, and clues, then respond with empathy and understanding. Be there for your dragon when they need comfort, reassurance, or assistance, and demonstrate that you are a trustworthy and reliable partner.

Bonding with your dragon is a dynamic and gratifying process that takes time, patience, and commitment. Spending quality time together, engaging in physical contact and affection, practicing clear and consistent communication, sharing meals and treats, exploring new environments together, playing games and engaging in enrichment activities, building trust through consistency and reliability, and listening and responding to your dragon's needs will strengthen your bond and create a strong and lasting connection with your dragon companion.

The Value of Mutual Respect

Mutual respect is the foundation of any meaningful relationship, including the one between you and your dragon friend. In this section, we will look at why mutual respect is essential for developing a strong and healthy relationship with your dragon.

Respecting your dragon involves acknowledging and honoring their uniqueness. Dragons, like people, have distinct personalities, interests, and eccentricities. Take the time to recognize and appreciate your dragon's distinct characteristics, and treat them as the unique individuals they are. By recognizing their uniqueness, you show respect for their autonomy and dignity.

Respecting your dragon's boundaries is crucial for establishing trust and a strong connection. Pay attention to your dragon's body language and cues, and honor their demand for privacy and autonomy. Avoid putting your dragon in situations that make them uncomfortable or anxious, and always ask for their permission before commencing physical contact or training exercises. Respecting your dragon's boundaries demonstrates that you prioritize their comfort and well-being over everything else.

Mutual respect is essential for effective communication, including listening and responding. Listen closely to your dragon's vocalizations, body language, and clues, and respond with empathy and understanding. Take the time to understand your dragon's needs, preferences, and feelings, and be available to them when they require comfort, reassurance, or assistance. By listening and responding to your dragon, you show that you value their opinions, feelings, and experiences.

Respecting your dragon involves allowing them to make choices and express themselves. Give your dragon options whenever feasible, whether it's choosing between different food, toys, or training exercises. Allow your dragon to express themselves in their own unique way while promoting autonomy and agency in all parts of their life. By giving your dragon choice and agency, you are empowering them and demonstrating your respect for their freedom to self-determination.

As the leader and guardian of your dragon, it's important to set a good example and show respect in all interactions. Treat your dragon with kindness, patience, and compassion, and demonstrate the behavior you want to see in return. Respect your dragon's emotions, needs, and boundaries, and seek to provide a safe and supportive atmosphere in which they feel cherished and appreciated. By leading with respect, you establish the foundation for a pleasant and mutually beneficial connection with your dragon.

Mutual respect is essential for establishing confidence and cooperation with your dragon. Respecting your dragon as a sentient being with thoughts and feelings fosters trust and lays the groundwork for a healthy and harmonious partnership. Respect is the foundation of good communication, collaboration, and partnership, allowing you and your dragon to work toward mutual goals and conquer difficulties as a team.

CHAPTER FIVE
Basic Training Commands:

In this chapter, we'll look at basic training commands that are necessary for establishing clear communication and laying a solid foundation of compliance and collaboration with your dragon companion. These basic commands serve as the foundation for more advanced training activities and are essential for maintaining a harmonious and well-behaved dragon.

1. Sit: The "sit" command instructs your dragon to sit on command. Begin by coaxing your dragon to a sitting position with a reward or target stick. As your dragon learns the order, associate the verbal signal "sit" with the desired behavior and reward them with praise and rewards for complying. To reinforce your dragon's comprehension and compliance, use the "sit" command in a variety of settings and situations.

2. Stay: The "stay" command instructs your dragon to remain in place until released. Begin by telling your dragon to sit or lie down, then provide the verbal cue "stay" while making a hand gesture to suggest that they should remain in place. Gradually expand the duration and

distance of your dragon's stay as they gain proficiency, always rewarding obedience. To improve your dragon's impulse control and reliability, practice the "stay" command in a variety of locations and distractions.

3. Come: The "come" command trains your dragon to return to you when summoned. Begin by calling your dragon's name, followed by the verbal signal "come" in a cheerful and welcoming tone. Use a gift or toy to entice your dragon back to you, and reward them liberally if they respond quickly. Practice the "come" command in safe, enclosed places first, then progressively introduce distractions and longer distances.

4. Down: The "down" command directs your dragon to lie down on the ground. Begin by instructing your dragon to sit, then use a treat or target stick to guide them to a laying position. Pair the verbal signal "down" with the desired behavior, then reward your dragon for compliance. Practice the "down" command on a regular basis to improve your dragon's understanding and fluency.

5. Leave It: The "leave it" command instructs your dragon to avoid interacting with or devouring unwanted items. Begin by offering an enticing toy or treat to your dragon and

instructing them to ignore it with the verbal signal "leave it". Redirect your dragon's attention to a more appropriate behavior or offer them a higher-value treat in exchange for obedience. To improve impulse control and self-control, practice the "leave it" command with a variety of objects and distractions.

6. Drop It: The "drop it" command releases an object from your dragon's mouth. Begin by giving your dragon a toy or object to hold, then use the verbal signal "drop it" to suggest a trade for a more desirable item or treat. Reward your dragon for following the command and freely releasing the object. Use the "drop it" command on a frequent basis to train your dragon to release stuff on cue and prevent resource guarding behavior.

7. Heel: The "heel" command encourages your dragon to walk calmly and carefully with you on a leash. Begin by utilizing the verbal cue "heel" and a hand signal to indicate the preferred position next to you. Encourage your dragon to stay in the appropriate position by rewarding them with goodies and praise for walking calmly beside you. Use the "heel" command for short walks or training sessions, gradually increasing the duration and distractions as your dragon develops.

Mastering these fundamental training commands is critical to building a solid foundation of obedience, communication, and cooperation with your dragon partner. Consistency, patience, and positive reinforcement are essential for success, so practice these instructions frequently and celebrate your dragon's development and accomplishments along the way. With devotion and commitment, you may establish a happy and fulfilling connection with your dragon based on trust, respect, and mutual understanding.

Training Your Dragon to Respond to Basic Commands

Teaching your dragon to listen to basic commands is a pleasurable and necessary part of training that promotes communication, obedience, and comprehension. In this section, we'll look at how to effectively teach your dragon to understand and obey simple orders.

1. Clear communication is essential for effective training. To communicate your expectations to your dragon, use simple, consistent verbal cues accompanied by appropriate hand signs or gestures. To avoid confusion, choose cues that are easy to recall and pronounce, and utilize them consistently throughout all training sessions.

2. Use Positive Reinforcement: Encouraging desired behaviors in your dragon through positive reinforcement is quite effective. Use food, praise, and other incentives to reinforce your dragon's responses to simple commands like sit, remain, and come. Reward your dragon soon after they complete the required behavior to reinforce the link between the command and the reward.

3. Break out commands into reasonable increments to help dragons grasp expectations. For example, while teaching the "sit" command,

begin by coaxing your dragon into a sitting position with a reward, then gradually remove the bait and depend exclusively on verbal cues and hand signals.

4. Patience and Consistency are essential for successful training. Understand that learning takes time, and your dragon may not learn commands overnight. Maintain patience with your dragon and provide moderate advice and encouragement during the learning process. Consistency in training methods, cues, and expectations will assist your dragon understand and reinforce their learning.

5. Regularly practice simple orders in different contexts to increase your dragon's learning and responsiveness. Begin training in a quiet, familiar setting with few distractions, then gradually increase the level of difficulty by introducing distractions such as other animals, noises, or unfamiliar circumstances. Practice in several areas to teach your dragon to respond to commands consistently in any situation.

6. Keep training sessions brief, entertaining, and engaging to keep your dragon interested and motivated. To avoid tiredness and boredom, alternate between short sessions throughout the

day. Incorporate play, games, and interactive activities into your training sessions to keep your dragon interested and engaged.

7. Be flexible and adapt to your dragon's needs. Be adaptable and tailor your training approach to your dragon's unique needs, personality, and learning style. If a certain command or tactic isn't working for your dragon, try a another strategy or divide the training into smaller chunks. Customize your training methods to fit your dragon's tastes and talents, and always prioritize their comfort and well-being.

Following these strategies and ideas will allow you to properly educate your dragon to answer to simple orders while also laying the framework for more sophisticated training sessions. Remember to be patient, consistent, and pleasant in your interactions with your dragon, and applaud their accomplishments along the way. With effort and perseverance, you can establish a strong and trusted connection with your dragon based on open communication, mutual respect, and cooperation.

Training Approaches for Obedience and Discipline

Establishing obedience and discipline in your dragon is critical for their safety, well-being, and peaceful life with you. In this section, we'll look at successful training methods that encourage compliance and discipline while maintaining a good and respectful connection with your dragon.

1. Positive Reinforcement: Effective obedience and discipline training relies heavily on positive reinforcement. This strategy involves rewarding

desired actions with sweets, praise, or other incentives, so reinforcing the link between the behavior and the reward. When your dragon follows a command or exhibits positive behavior, treat them immediately to reinforce their understanding and motivation to repeat the activity.

2. Establishing obedience and discipline in your dragon requires consistent and repetitive training. Use consistent verbal cues, physical gestures, and expectations during all training sessions to prevent confusion and enhance learning. Regular training activities can help your dragon internalize commands and acquire excellent habits. Maintaining obedience and discipline over time requires consistent practice.

3. Effective instruction and discipline require clear communication. Use straightforward, precise verbal cues and hand signs to communicate your expectations to your dragon. Maintain consistency in your commands and expectations, and avoid using vague or confusing language. Before giving your dragon directions, make sure they understand what is expected of them, and provide explicit advice and feedback during training sessions.

4. Establish clear boundaries and regulations to promote obedience and discipline in your dragon. Clearly identify acceptable and undesirable actions, and regularly enforce these standards via positive reward and redirection. When establishing boundaries, be tough but fair, and do not penalize your dragon for mistakes or misunderstandings. Consistency is essential for establishing boundaries and developing obedience.

5. Incorporate training games and challenges into your routine to improve your dragon's obedience and discipline. Use interactive games, puzzles, and obstacle courses to engage your dragon's mind and body while reinforcing training orders and behaviors. Make your dragon's training sessions entertaining and rewarding in order to encourage active involvement and collaboration.

6. Timeouts and Corrections: While positive reinforcement is the primary strategy for promoting compliance and discipline, it may be essential to use timeouts or corrections to address negative actions. Use timeouts sparingly and as a last resort, and keep them brief and non-punitive. After a timeout, refocus your dragon's attention on more suitable behaviors and promote desired behaviors with positive

reinforcement.

7. Patience and Understanding: These traits are crucial for effective instruction and discipline. Recognize that learning takes time, and your dragon may make mistakes along the way. Be patient with your dragon, and offer gentle advice and support as it learns and grows. Maintain a pleasant and respectful connection with your dragon, and refrain from employing punishment or harsh techniques that could erode trust and obedience.

By using these obedience and discipline training methods, you may help your dragon develop a strong foundation of respect, cooperation, and mutual understanding. Remember to be patient, consistent, and pleasant in your interactions with your dragon, and applaud its progress and accomplishments along the way. With effort and perseverance, you may raise a well-behaved and obedient dragon companion who enhances your life with devotion, camaraderie, and affection.

Positive Reinforcement Techniques

Positive reinforcement strategies are effective tools for encouraging desired behaviors while also developing a deep sense of trust and collaboration with your dragon companion. In this section, we'll look at several positive reinforcement tactics that you can utilize to properly train and promote compliance in your dragon.

1. Treats and Rewards: Providing treats and rewards is a popular and successful method of positive reinforcement. Use small, bite-sized goodies that your dragon enjoys as rewards for desired actions like sitting, staying, arriving when called, and more. When your dragon appropriately reacts to commands, show it plenty of praise and food, and progressively reduce the frequency of treats as the behavior improves.

2. Positive reinforcement, such as verbal praise and tenderness, can deepen the link with your dragon. When your dragon obeys directions or exhibits desired behaviors, praise them with a pleasant and enthusiastic tone of voice. Shower them with love words, gentle patting, and scratches in their favorite locations to encourage their obedience and make training sessions more pleasurable and gratifying.

3. Clicker Training: This positive reward strategy involves using a handheld clicker to mark desired behaviors. Begin by linking the sound of the clicker with rewards by clicking and immediately providing a treat to your dragon. Then, use the clicker to encourage specific behaviors or actions, followed by a treat as a reward. Clicker training helps your dragon understand which behaviors are rewarded and can accelerate the learning process.

4. Target Training: This positive reinforcement strategy trains your dragon to contact a specific object, such a target stick or your hand, with their nose or paw. Begin by introducing the target object to your dragon and rewarding them with treats whenever they contact it. Gradually mold the behavior by shifting the target object to different places or heights and paying your dragon for following it. Target training can be used to teach a variety of behaviors and

commands, including walking on a leash and performing tricks.

5. Incorporating play and interactive games in training sessions reinforces obedience and strengthens the link with your dragon. Toys, balls, and other interactive objects can help your dragon's natural instincts and provide mental stimulation. Play games like fetch, tug-of-war, or hide-and-seek to teach your dragon to obey directions and display desired behaviors while having fun.

6. Environmental Rewards: Environmental rewards are natural reinforcers found in your dragon's habitat, such as access to a favorite resting location, exploration of new surroundings, or social interactions with other animals or humans. Use these environmental rewards wisely to reinforce desired behaviors and encourage your dragon to follow directions. Allow your dragon to go for a walk or explore a new area as a reward for good training behavior.

7. Effective positive reinforcement relies on consistency and timing. Be constant in your use of rewards and praise, and always reward your dragon right away when they demonstrate the desired behavior. Timing is crucial because your dragon must associate the reward with the exact behavior you're encouraging. To properly

reinforce a behavior, use a marker phrase or clicker to signify the exact instant it occurs, followed by a prompt reward.

Incorporating these positive reinforcement tactics into your training regimen allows you to effectively encourage obedience and reinforce desired actions in your dragon while also deepening your bond. Remember to be patient, consistent, and generous with rewards, and to recognize your dragon's development and accomplishments along the way. With commitment and positive reinforcement, you may raise a well-behaved and responsive dragon friend who enhances your life with devotion, camaraderie, and love.

CHAPTER SIX
Advanced Training Techniques

In this chapter, we'll look at advanced training approaches for challenging and stimulating your dragon partner both mentally and physically. These approaches extend beyond simple obedience orders, allowing you to improve your dragon's skills, intelligence, and agility while building your bond via shared learning experiences.

1. Targeting and influencing: These sophisticated training techniques educate dragons to do certain behaviors by gradually influencing their activities towards a desired goal. Begin by assigning a target activity, such as touching a target stick with their nose or paw, and rewarding incremental progress toward that action. Shape your dragon's activities using progressive approximations, rewarding each step toward the goal behavior until they reach the intended result.

2. Agility and Obstacle Courses: These courses can improve your dragon's physical and mental agility, while also rewarding obedience and focus. Create a course with tunnels, hoops, weave poles, and other obstacles, then direct your dragon through it using verbal cues and

hand signals. Encourage your dragon to negotiate the course quickly and precisely, rewarding them for successfully completing each obstacle.

3. Advanced Trick Training: Teach your dragon a range of spectacular and entertaining tricks to demonstrate their intelligence and flexibility. Teach tricks like fetching objects, waving, rolling over, acting dead, and even imitating human actions. Break down each trick into smaller steps and use positive reinforcement to help your dragon master each one before moving on to the next.

4. Off-Leash Training: Teach your dragon to respond reliably to directions without a leash or confinement. Begin by practicing obedience commands like come, remain, and heel in a safe, confined environment with few distractions. Gradually increase the difficulty level by introducing distractions and practicing in various settings until your dragon can reliably obey commands off-leash.

5. Clicker Training for Complex Behaviors: Clicker training simplifies complex behaviors and sequences into simple steps. Use the clicker to indicate each step toward the desired behavior and reward your dragon for their efforts. Break down complex behaviors like opening doors,

fetching specific items, or completing trick sequences, and then use clicker training to reinforce each step.

6. Engage and challenge your dragon with mental stimulation activities, especially if they are intelligent or energetic. Include activities like puzzle toys, food puzzles, fragrance games, or interactive games that involve problem-solving and critical thinking abilities. Give your dragon opportunity to use their natural instincts and intelligence in a positive and gratifying way.

7. Freestyle Training and Performance: Showcase your dragon's talents and personality with choreographed dances paired to music or narration. Create a routine that shows your dragon's strengths and abilities, using a range of tricks, behaviors, and movements. Practice the routine on a regular basis, honing and polishing each part to provide a smooth and appealing performance.

These advanced training approaches provide exciting possibilities for you and your dragon to learn and grow together, thereby strengthening your bond via shared experiences. Remember to train your dragon with patience, positivity, and consistency, and to appreciate his or her development and triumphs along the way. With devotion and commitment to sophisticated training techniques, you'll be able to maximize your dragon's potential and have a fulfilling and enriching partnership for years to come.

Developing Specialized Skills and Abilities for Your Dragon

Developing specialized skills and abilities in your dragon can lead to new possibilities for enrichment, fulfillment, and practical uses. In this section, we'll look at how to find, cultivate, and refine specialized skills and abilities based on your dragon's specific capabilities and interests.

1. Determine Your Dragon's Strengths and

Interests:
Begin by evaluating your dragon's strengths, hobbies, and natural abilities to find areas for skill growth. Observe their behavior, reactions, and preferences in a variety of activities, taking note of any specific talents or behaviors in which they excel or are interested. This will provide crucial information on areas in which your dragon may have a natural ability or inclination.

2. Establish Clear Goals and Objectives: After identifying areas for skill development, create measurable goals to drive training activities. Define the precise skills or abilities you want your dragon to develop, as well as milestones and benchmarks for tracking their growth. Break down larger goals into smaller, more manageable steps to improve learning and maintain consistent progress toward mastery.

3. Customising Training Methods and Techniques:
Customize your training methods and strategies to match the unique skills and abilities you want to develop in your dragon. Investigate and test specialized training methods and procedures that are relevant to your objectives, such as agility training, scent work, flying training, or specialized task training. Adapt your training methods to your dragon's individual learning style, personality, and preferences.

4. Mastering specific skills requires consistent practice and repetition. Regular training sessions should be dedicated to strengthening your dragon's particular skills, with an emphasis on reinforcing desired behaviors and perfecting procedures. Practice each talent or ability in a variety of contexts and environments to help it generalize and be reliable in real-world circumstances.

5. Fostering Enriching and Stimulating Environments: Create environments that encourage the growth of particular skills and abilities in your dragon. Encourage learning and skill development by providing chances for exploration, problem solving, and engagement with novel stimuli. Provide a range of engaging toys, puzzles, and enrichment activities to test your dragon's thinking and encourage them to apply their specific skills constructively.

6. Seek Expert Guidance and Support: Consult skilled trainers, behaviorists, or professionals who specialize in the talents you want to develop in your dragon. Consult with competent persons or attend specialized training classes or seminars that are specific to your preferred area of competence. Learn from their thoughts, recommendations, and tactics to improve your training methods and speed up your dragon's

advancement.

7. Celebrate your dragon's growth as they gain specific skills and abilities. Recognize and reward their efforts with praise, candy, or other incentives to boost motivation and confidence. Celebrate milestones and successes along the road, and reflect on your dragon's progress in skill development and growth.

By using these tactics for developing specialized skills and abilities in your dragon, you may help them reach their full potential and become a well-rounded and versatile friend. Accept the road of learning and growth together, and embrace the distinct qualities and abilities that your dragon brings to your shared travels and experiences.

Agility Training

Agility training is a dynamic and exciting sport that tests your dragon's physical talents, mental acuity, and coordination while building your bond via collaboration and communication. In this section, we will look at the ideas and practices of agility training, as well as how to include this fun discipline into your dragon's daily routine.

1. Understanding Agility Training: Agility training involves traversing obstacles like tunnels, jumps, and weave poles in a timed and controlled manner. The goal is to finish the course fast and precisely, while adhering to the handler's cues and orders. Agility training increases your dragon's physical fitness and coordination while also increasing their attention, confidence, and problem-solving abilities.

2. Getting Started with Agility Equipment:

Introduce your dragon to basic agility equipment in a safe and controlled setting. Begin with low-impact obstacles like modest jumps or tunnels, gradually increasing in complexity and difficulty as your dragon acquires confidence and expertise. Positive reinforcement strategies such as rewards, praise, and play can help your dragon explore and interact with the equipment freely.

3. Teach Foundation Skills: Before tackling a complete agility course, teach your dragon foundation skills including aiming, hind-end awareness, and directional cuing. Targeting is the process of teaching your dragon to touch a specific object, such as a target stick or your hand, with their nose or paw. Hind-end awareness activities help your dragon develop balance, coordination, and control over their back end, which is essential for successfully traversing obstacles. Directional cues like "left," "right," "wait," and "go" are critical for steering your dragon through the agility course with precision and accuracy.

4. Developing Confidence and Trust: Agility training can be scary for certain dragons, particularly those who are shy or easily startled by unexpected stimuli. Develop your dragon's confidence and trust gradually by exposing them to agility equipment in a positive and supportive environment. Use desensitization strategies to

assist your dragon become accustomed to the sights, sounds, and sensations connected with agility training. Provide plenty of praise, reassurance, and prizes to boost your dragon's confidence and motivation to overcome obstacles.

5. Practice Agility Skills: After your dragon has mastered fundamental skills and gained confidence with agility equipment, begin training in a structured and controlled environment. Create a simple agility course with a variety of obstacles and difficulties, then guide your dragon through it using verbal cues, hand signs, and body language. Focus on reinforcing desired behaviors and rewarding your dragon's efforts, even if they make mistakes or face setbacks.

6. Progressing to Advanced Agility: As your dragon improves in agility training, gradually raise the course complexity and difficulty to keep them involved and challenged. Introduce more obstacles, increase the speed and distance challenges, and include more complex maneuvers like tight turns, serpentines, and handling skills. Practice consistently to enhance your dragon's agility, speed, and precision.

7. Fostering Teamwork and Communication: Agility training promotes collaboration and communication between you and your dragon.

Collaborate to traverse the course, anticipate each other's motions, and overcome obstacles with ease and precision. Use clear, consistent cues and signals to direct your dragon through the course, and celebrate each successful run as proof of your collaboration and mutual understanding.

By introducing agility training into your dragon's daily routine, you can give them a fun and challenging outlet for their physical and mental energy, while also building your bond through shared experiences and triumphs. Accept the challenge of agility training together and experience the pleasure of learning new skills and overcoming difficulties as a group.

Combat Training

Combat training is a particular type of education that prepares your dragon for future fights or defensive scenarios. While not necessary for all dragons, combat training may be required for those who serve in protective duties, such as guard dragons, or who live in areas where they may confront threats or predators.

1. Defensive moves: Combat training teaches dragons defensive moves to protect themselves and their territory. This could include strategies like shielding, dodging, and evasive moves to evade oncoming attacks or dangers.

2. Offensive Techniques: In addition to defensive measures, fighting training may incorporate offensive techniques to prevent or neutralize threats. This could include teaching your dragon how to strike, grapple, or bite successfully in the event that they need to protect themselves.

3. Combat training focuses on increasing your dragon's tactical awareness and decision-making abilities in high-pressure situations. This may include scenario-based training exercises that imitate real-world hazards and need your dragon to assess and respond appropriately.

4. Controlled Engagement: Combat training teaches dragons to use force as a last resort. This includes teaching your dragon to recognize dangers and display warning signals before engaging in physical combat.

5. Obedience and Discipline: Good fighting training involves both obedience and discipline. Your dragon must respond to commands even in stressful or risky conditions in order to be properly directed and prevent unnecessary risks.

6. Stress Management: Combat training teaches stress management skills to help dragons stay calm and focused during stressful situations. Desensitization exercises, relaxation techniques, and positive reinforcement may all be used to help improve resilience and confidence.

7. Safety Protocols: Combat training focuses on safety at all times. To reduce the danger of injury to your dragon and those engaged, ensure that training sessions are undertaken under the guidance of competent professionals in controlled surroundings.

While combat training is not appropriate for all dragons, it is critical for those in roles that require it to ensure their safety and efficacy in carrying out their tasks. Approach battle training with prudence and remember to emphasize your dragon's well-being throughout the process.

CHAPTER SEVEN
Troubleshooting Common Problems

In this chapter, we will discuss frequent issues and obstacles that may arise during your dragon training journey, as well as practical answers and troubleshooting tactics to help you overcome them. From behavior difficulties to training setbacks, this chapter will provide you with the knowledge and resources you need to properly manage common obstacles and ensure a successful training experience for you and your dragon.

1. **Problem:** A lack of motivation or engagement.

Solution: Determine what motivates your dragon, such as food, toys, praise, or play, and utilize these incentives to encourage participation in training sessions. Make training enjoyable and interesting by adding interactive activities, variety, and positive reinforcement approaches.
2. **Issue:** Difficulty with Recall or Command Compliance.

Solution: Review and reinforce fundamental

obedience training to ensure that your dragon knows and consistently answers to important instructions like come, stay, and leave it. Increase the value of compliance prizes and practice commands in low-distraction areas before gradually introducing distractions.

3. **Problem:** Fear or Anxiety in Training Settings

Solution: Develop a secure and supportive training environment for your dragon by gradually desensitizing it to any triggers or stressors. Counterconditioning approaches can help your dragon adjust its emotional response to fear-inducing events and gain confidence through pleasant experiences.

4. **Issue**: Resource Guarding or Aggression

Solution: To address resource guarding behavior, train your dragon to associate the presence of people near valued resources with good consequences like rewards or attention. Implement guidelines for properly handling and redirecting aggressive behavior, and consult with a professional behaviorist as needed.
5. **Problem**: Lack of progress or plateau in training.

Solution: To assist learning and avoid overwhelm, break complex behaviors down into smaller, more manageable steps. To keep sessions interesting and prevent boredom, experiment with different training methodologies and venues. Be patient and persistent, recognizing tiny triumphs and keeping a positive outlook on development.

6. **Problem**: Destructive or unwanted habits.

Solution: Determine and treat the root causes of harmful behavior, such as boredom, worry, or a lack of stimulation. Enrichment activities and toys can serve as acceptable outlets for natural behaviors like as chewing or digging. Positive reinforcement can be used to redirect undesirable behaviors and encourage desirable behaviors.

7. **Problem**: Communication breakdowns or misunderstandings

Solution: Improve communication between you and your dragon by adjusting your training cues and signals to ensure clarity and consistency. Take the time to learn your dragon's body language and vocalizations, and then respond accordingly to their demands and signals. Create a solid foundation of trust and mutual understanding by engaging in consistent, positive encounters.

By proactively addressing frequent concerns and

applying efficient troubleshooting procedures, you can overcome barriers and succeed in your dragon training efforts. Remember to tackle problems with patience, empathy, and an openness to changing your strategy as needed to guarantee a happy and rewarding training experience for both you and your dragon.

Addressing Disobedience and Aggression

Dealing with your dragon's disobedience and hostility might be difficult, but it is necessary for the relationship to remain secure and happy. In this section, we will look at successful techniques for dealing with these behaviors through patience, understanding, and positive reinforcement.

1. Understanding the Root Causes: Dragons may

exhibit disobedience and aggressiveness due to fear, insecurity, territoriality, or dissatisfaction. Take the time to examine the situation and discover any potential triggers or stressors that could be influencing your dragon's behavior.

2. Implementing Consistent Training: Effectively managing disobedience and violence requires consistent training. Regularly reinforce obedience training, emphasizing key instructions like "sit," "stay," and "leave it." Use positive reinforcement tactics to encourage desired behaviors while discouraging unwanted ones.

3. Addressing Fear and Insecurity: To address disobedience or violence caused by fear or insecurity, gradually build your dragon's confidence and trust using desensitization and counterconditioning techniques. Make positive associations with previously feared stimuli by combining them with incentives or enjoyable experiences.

4. Establish clear boundaries and enforce them regularly to prevent disobedience and hostility. To deal with misbehavior quickly, use stern but reasonable corrective strategies such as refocusing your dragon's attention or temporarily revoking privileges.

5. Avoiding Triggers and Provocations: Identify

potential triggers or events that may cause anger in your dragon and take proactive measures to prevent or lessen them. Create a peaceful and predictable environment for your dragon, reducing stressors and disputes that may cause aggressive behavior.

6. Seeking Professional Guidance: If disobedience or aggressiveness persists, see a licensed animal behaviorist or experienced trainer. They can offer individualized advise and behavior modification approaches based on your dragon's unique requirements and issues.

7. Prioritizing Safety and Well-being: Prioritize the safety and well-being of yourself, your dragon, and those around you. Avoid escalating conflicts or using punitive measures that could exacerbate aggression. Instead, use de-escalation tactics and positive reinforcement to encourage serenity and cooperation.

By dealing with disobedience and aggression with patience, consistency, and positive reinforcement, you may effectively manage these difficult behaviors while also cultivating a trusting and respectful connection with your dragon. Remember to handle each scenario with respect and compassion, and to recognize accomplishments and improvements along the way.

Managing Fear and Anxiety
in Dragons

Fear and worry can have a substantial impact on a dragon's health and behavior, limiting its capacity to learn, socialize, and grow. In this section, we'll look at how to detect, handle, and alleviate fear and anxiety in dragons using compassion and understanding.

1. Recognizing Fear and Anxiety: Identify indications of fear and anxiety in your dragon, including as shivering, hiding, pacing, vocalizing, or aggressive behavior. Pay attention to your dragon's body language and behavior to identify potential stressors.

2. Creating a Safe Environment: Ensure your dragon's safety by reducing stressors and offering comfort and reassurance. Ensure easy access to hiding places, cozy retreats, and familiar objects that provide a sense of security and predictability.

3. Gradual Desensitization: By gradually introducing your dragon to frightened stimuli or circumstances, they might gain confidence over time. Begin with low-level exposure and gradually increase the intensity or duration as your dragon grows more comfortable.

4. Counterconditioning Techniques: To change your dragon's emotional response to frightened

stimuli, couple them with good experiences or incentives. Create positive connections with previously feared stimuli through food, praise, or play to reduce fear and anxiety.

5. Applying Relaxation Techniques:
Teach your dragon relaxation practices like deep breathing exercises, muscle relaxation, and relaxing massages to help them cope with stress and anxiety. To induce relaxation and relieve tension, create a peaceful environment by playing soothing music, dimming the lighting or using aromatherapy.

6. Create consistent routines and timetables for your dragon to lessen worry and increase security. Maintain consistent meal times, exercise regimens, and sleep habits to foster a secure and reassuring atmosphere.

7. Seeking Professional Support: If fear and anxiety persist, see a trained veterinarian or animal behaviorist with expertise in dragon behavior. They can offer expert advice, behavior modification strategies, and medication alternatives to assist your dragon manage anxiety and improve its quality of life.

8. Approach fear and worry in dragons with patience, compassion, and empathy. Recognize that conquering fear and anxiety takes time and

may necessitate trial and error to determine the best effective tactics for your specific dragon. Be encouraging and soothing as your dragon learns to overcome their anxieties.

By treating dragon fear and anxiety with kindness, understanding, and proactive involvement, you may help them feel safe, comfortable, and confident in their surroundings. Remember to applaud your dragon's growth and improvements throughout the road, and recognize the perseverance and courage required to conquer their phobias.

Health Concerns and Veterinary Care

Maintaining your dragon's health is essential for their overall well-being and lifespan. In this section, we'll go over typical health issues in dragons and the importance of veterinarian care in keeping them healthy and happy.

1. Regularly monitor your dragon's health, including behavior, eating, and physical appearance. Look for symptoms of disease or discomfort, such as changes in eating patterns, lethargy, unusual droppings, or respiratory problems. Regular health check-ups with a skilled reptile veterinarian are critical for detecting and treating health issues early.

2. Nutrition and Diet: Give your dragon a balanced and nutritious diet based on their species, age, and size. Provide a range of fresh vegetables, fruits, and high-quality commercial diets designed exclusively for dragons. Avoid

giving your dragon poisonous or improper items, such as pesticide-treated insects or high-fat or sugar-containing diets.

3. Environmental Factors: Ensure your dragon's habitat fulfills their individual needs, such as temperature, humidity, lighting, and substrate. Monitor environmental conditions on a regular basis and make modifications as needed to ensure optimal health and comfort. Provide hiding places, basking spaces, and plenty of room for physical exercise to encourage natural behaviors and cerebral stimulation.

4. Parasite Prevention and Control: Untreated parasites, including internal worms and external mites, can pose serious health threats to dragons. To reduce the danger of parasitic infestations, follow your veterinarian's recommendations for a frequent parasite prevention program that includes fecal checks, deworming medications, and environmental cleanliness measures.

5. Routine Veterinary Examinations and Preventive Care: Regularly examine your dragon for overall health and early detection of any medical disorders. Your veterinarian can advise you on preventive care methods like immunizations, parasite management, and dental treatment to keep your dragon healthy and avoid potential health issues.

6. Prepare for Emergencies: Familiarize yourself with typical health emergencies in dragons and know how to respond quickly. Have a reptile-friendly veterinarian or emergency clinic on call in case of an emergency, and maintain a first-aid box supplied with supplies for minor injuries or diseases.

7. Educate Yourself: Research trusted sources from veterinary specialists and herpetological organizations to learn about typical health concerns, husbandry techniques, and preventive care measures for dragons. Attend educational courses, seminars, or online forums to broaden your knowledge and improve your ability to give the best care for your dragon.

8. Establish a Trusting and Collaborative Relationship with Your Veterinarian: Your reptile veterinarian can provide vital counsel, support, and medical care for your dragon throughout its life. Communicate freely and proactively with your veterinarian about any health issues or questions you may have, and follow their advice for keeping your dragon healthy and well.

Prioritizing your dragon's health and investing in preventive care and veterinarian support can let them to enjoy a long, healthy, and fulfilling life.

Remember that proactive health management and frequent veterinary treatment are key components of responsible dragon ownership, as they contribute to your scaly companion's general happiness and health.

CHAPTER EIGHT

Beyond Training: The Dragon-Human Partnership

In this last chapter, we'll look at the deeper

aspects of the dragon-human interaction that go beyond simple training tactics. We'll look at the emotional connection, mutual understanding, and shared experiences that constitute dragons' special link with their human partners.

1. Building Trust and Mutual Respect: The dragon-human partnership relies on trust and respect. Building a solid foundation of trust requires time, patience, and continuous positive encounters. Respect your dragon's boundaries, preferences, and uniqueness, and they will respond with devotion, cooperation, and affection.

2. Fostering Emotional Bonds: The link between a dragon and its human companion extends beyond obedience and training. It is a strong emotional bond built on empathy, camaraderie, and shared experiences. Nurture this emotional connection by spending quality time together, engaging in meaningful exchanges, and doing acts of compassion and affection.

3. Promoting Communication and Understanding: Dragons and people communicate through nonverbal clues and directives. It entails recognizing and comprehending each other's body language, vocalizations, and nonverbal clues. Learn to listen to your dragon's wants, desires, and

emotions while also communicating your own thoughts and feelings clearly and empathically.

4. Sharing Adventures and Experiences: The dragon-human collaboration fosters the delight of sharing adventures and experiences. Whether you're exploring the great outdoors, embarking on trips of discovery, or simply enjoying each other's company at home, treasure these shared moments and create lasting memories that enrich your relationship.

5. Fostering Growth and Development: The dragon-human partnership promotes growth and development for both parties. Encourage your dragon's physical, mental, and emotional well-being through training, enrichment, and positive reinforcement. Allow yourself to develop and learn alongside your dragon, facing new difficulties and experiences together.

6. Celebrating Individuality and Diversity: Each dragon-human connection is unique, influenced by their personalities, histories, and situations. Celebrate the uniqueness and diversity of your partnership, acknowledging each other's strengths, idiosyncrasies, and differences and appreciating the richness they contribute to your shared experiences.

7. Honoring the holy Bond: The dragon-human

collaboration is a holy bond that crosses species and linguistic barriers. It is a partnership based on love, trust, and mutual respect, and it should be valued and treasured as such. Treat your dragon as a valued companion and equal partner on your path through life.

To summarize, the dragon-human connection is a profound and significant relationship that benefits both sides in numerous ways. Beyond training tactics and obedience instructions, it is a voyage of connection, understanding, and mutual growth that transcends the mundane and transforms lives. Accept the beauty and depth of your relationship with your dragon, and treasure the limitless possibilities for a lifetime of love, companionship, and adventure.

The roles of Dragons in Society

Dragons have played a wide range of roles in communities throughout history, from mythical creatures of folklore to treasured friends and protectors today. In this section, we'll look at the various roles dragons play in society, as well as their influence on culture, folklore, and daily life.

1. Cultural and Mythological Significance: Dragons are widely represented in various cultures' mythology and folklore. They represent power and wisdom, and they frequently function as guardians of treasure or information. In many religions, dragons are adored as divine beings or supernatural forces, signifying both beneficent and malevolent forces depending on the context.

2. Dragons as Guardians and Protectors: In some cultures, dragons are thought to safeguard people, places, and valuables from danger. They are frequently portrayed as noble and majestic creatures, passionately loyal to those they believe are worthy of their care. There are

numerous stories about dragons protecting kingdoms, temples, and sacred locations from invaders or natural disasters.

3. Companions and Allies: Dragons are commonly depicted as human companions and allies, forging strong friendships and collaboration. They may help people with a variety of tasks, such as exploration, transportation, and even as therapy animals, providing emotional support and companionship.

4. Dragons are often depicted as icons of strength, fortitude, and resilience in art, literature, and culture. They appear frequently in fantasy novels, films, and artwork, captivating audiences worldwide with their majestic beauty and awe-inspiring presence.

5. Economic and Commercial Significance: Dragons have economic and commercial value, especially in areas where they are recognized as tourist attractions or cultural symbols. Dragon-themed festivals, events, and goods can benefit local economies and tourism industries by generating cash and instilling communal pride.

6. Environmental and Conservation Perspectives: Dragons can promote wildlife conservation and habitat preservation. Dragons can motivate people to take action to protect nature and

biodiversity for future generations by increasing awareness of endangered species and habitats.

7. Ethical and Moral Considerations: The portrayal of dragons in literature, culture, and entertainment can reflect societal attitudes towards animals and the environment. Advocates may utilize dragon imagery and symbolism to convey themes of compassion, empathy, and stewardship for all living things.

In short, dragons play a wide range of roles in civilization, from mythological creatures of folklore to cherished companions and cultural emblems. Their effect extends beyond fantasy and fiction, influencing our views, ideals, and goals in profound and significant ways. By recognizing dragons' rich cultural heritage and symbolism, we can celebrate their enduring legacy while also appreciating the enchantment and wonder they contribute to our world.

Working with Your Dragon for Mutual Benefit.

Human-dragon alliances are more than just companionship; they are about teamwork and mutual benefit. In this section, we'll look at how collaborating with your dragon can lead to mutual development, fulfillment, and success.

1. Determine your dragon's skills, abilities, and natural gifts. Recognize what makes your dragon unique, and how their powers can compliment your own.

2. Aligning Goals and Objectives: Identify areas where your interests coincide to align your goals

and objectives. Set common goals that both you and your dragon can work toward, whether it's exploring new territory, overcoming obstacles, or reaching personal milestones.

3. Collaborative Problem-Solving: Utilize teamwork to resolve challenges. Your dragon's distinct perspective and abilities may provide new ideas and innovative solutions to problems you confront. Encourage teamwork and open communication in order to efficiently solve difficulties together.

4. Division of Labor: Achieve a balanced partnership by assigning tasks and responsibilities depending on each party's strengths and abilities. Recognize and respect your dragon's unique contributions to the table, whether they are protecting, scouting, or offering emotional support.

5. Encourage shared learning and growth by consistently challenging yourself to expand your knowledge, skills, and capabilities. Whether you're learning new training techniques, exploring new environments, or mastering new talents together, see each event as an opportunity for mutual growth and development.

6. Recognize and celebrate victories and milestones with your dragon. Whether it's a

successful training session, a significant achievement, or a shared experience, take the time to recognize your accomplishments and the link that brought you together.

7. Maintaining Balance and Harmony: Respect each other's limits, needs, and well-being in your partnership. Avoid overworking or exploiting your dragon, and focus on their health, happiness, and quality of life. Create a connection based on trust, respect, and reciprocity, in which both sides gain from the collaboration.

Working together with your dragon for mutual advantage allows you to maximize your partnership's potential and achieve incredible feats. Accept teamwork, communication, and common goals, and allow the power of your partnership carry you to new heights of success, contentment, and pleasure.

The Future of Dragon Training

As we look ahead, the future of dragon training promises exciting possibilities and potential breakthroughs that will change the way we engage with these wonderful beasts. In this section, we'll look at how rising trends, technologies, and ethical considerations are changing the future of dragon training.

1. Future Training strategies: Innovative strategies based on behavioral science, neurology, and animal cognition studies may be developed for dragon training. These tactics may use positive reinforcement, enrichment, and cognitive training methods to improve human-dragon communication, comprehension, and collaboration.

2. Technology Integration: Technology can enhance dragon training by creating specific tools, equipment, and digital platforms for communication, training, and data analysis. Virtual reality simulations, augmented reality interfaces, and wearable gadgets may provide new ways to connect with dragons while improving training outcomes.

3. Ethical Considerations and Welfare Standards: As our understanding of animal welfare and ethics evolves, dragon training may prioritize the well-being and welfare of dragons over other factors. Consent, autonomy, and freedom of choice are all ethical concerns that can influence training techniques and standards, ensuring that dragons are treated with respect, dignity, and compassion throughout their training.

4. Integrating Conservation and Environmental

Education: In the future, dragon training may prioritize conservation and environmental education, emphasizing the need to protect wild dragon species and habitats. To foster a better understanding of dragons and their ecological significance, training programs may include themes such as conservation awareness, sustainability, and ecosystem management.

5. Cultural Exchange and Collaboration: As the globe becomes more interconnected, dragon training may benefit from cultural exchange and collaboration among teachers, enthusiasts, and academics from many backgrounds and places. By sharing knowledge, techniques, and best practices, we can broaden the field of dragon training and create greater understanding and admiration for these amazing creatures across cultures and boundaries.

6. Exploration of New Frontiers: Dragon training could expand beyond Earth to include extraterrestrial expeditions, habitat exploration, and settlement. Dragons, with their flexibility, intelligence, and resilience, could be ideal partners and collaborators in humanity's quest to discover the universe.

7. Innovation and Adaptation: To influence the future of dragon training, trainers, academics, and enthusiasts must continue to innovate and

collaborate. By embracing new ideas, technology, and ethical principles, we may ensure that dragon training progresses in ways that benefit the well-being, understanding, and coexistence of people and dragons for future generations.

To summarize, the future of dragon training offers limitless prospects for innovation, collaboration, and ethical growth. By embracing evolving trends, technologies, and ethical issues, we may create a future in which humans and dragons coexist peacefully, recognizing each other's distinct abilities, viewpoints, and contributions to the world. As we embark on this voyage into the future, let us envisage a world in which the link between people and dragons inspires wonder, astonishment, and discovery for future generations.

CHAPTER NINE

Stories of Success

This chapter will explore amazing success stories from dragon trainers and their scaly partners. These stories demonstrate the transformational potential of the dragon-human connection, as well as the astounding achievements that can be accomplished with dedication, perseverance, and mutual trust.

1. **The Story of Valor and Bravery:**
Meet Aria and her dragon, Ember, a brave duo on a quest to save their village from a terrifying predator. Aria and Ember triumphed over their concerns thanks to tireless training and unrelenting resolve, earning their community's admiration and gratitude.

2. **The voyage of Discovery and Exploration**:
Join Kai and his dragon, Luna, on an epic voyage of discovery and exploration through

undiscovered lands, uncovering hidden treasures. Together, Kai and Luna endured harsh terrain, solved ancient secrets, and formed unbreakable relationships that crossed time and space.

3. **The Triumph of Perseverance and Resilience**: Follow Maya and her dragon, Storm, as they overcome apparently insurmountable difficulties to achieve victory. Despite numerous setbacks, Maya and Storm remained steady in their commitment, deriving strength from their profound friendship and unflinching faith in one another.

4. **The Legacy of Wisdom and Guidance**: Learn about Elder Dragon Arion, a wise guardian who passed down significant knowledge to generations of dragon trainers. Arion's lessons and counsel encouraged countless people to go on their own paths of self-discovery and enlightenment.

5. **The bond of friendship and companionship**: Experience the inspiring story of Sarah and her dragon, Blaze, whose friendship transcends species and linguistic barriers. Sarah and Blaze exchanged laughter, sorrow, and innumerable adventures, demonstrating that genuine friendship has no limitations.

6. **The Quest for Harmony and Balance**: Alex

and his dragon, Zephyr, seek harmony and balance in a world divided by conflict and strife. Alex and Zephyr's unrelenting devotion to peace and understanding brought warring tribes together and restored harmony to the country, creating a legacy of hope and healing.

7. **The Triumph of Love and Sacrifice**. Witness the story of Elena and her dragon, Midnight, whose love and sacrifice crossed the lines of life and death. In the midst of overwhelming darkness, Elena and Midnight's love illuminated the way forward, leading them to a brighter future full of hope and atonement.

These success tales serve as reminders of the transformational power of the dragon-human connection, as well as the unlimited potential that each of us possesses. May these stories inspire and motivate us, encouraging us to embrace the links of friendship, courage, and compassion that connect us to our dragon companions on our journey through life.

Inspirational Stories of Successful Dragon Trainers.

In this part, we'll look at inspirational stories about dragon trainers who have achieved incredible success through devotion, enthusiasm, and a strong bond with their scaly friends. These stories demonstrate the transformational power of the dragon-human link and are a source of inspiration for aspiring trainers worldwide.

1. **The Journey of Redemption**: Jackson, a former dragon poacher, became a conservationist

after encountering a wounded dragon in the wild. Determined to make amends, Jackson dedicated himself to conserving dragons and their habitats, eventually becoming a global leader in dragon conservation.

2. The Triumph of Trust and Understanding: Join Lily, a young trainer with an aptitude for connecting with dragons, on her quest to rehabilitate a traumatized dragon released from captivity. Lily earns the dragon's trust and helps them overcome their past suffering with patience, empathy, and steadfast trust, demonstrating that love and understanding can heal even the darkest wounds.

3. The Bond of Healing and Hope: This wonderful narrative follows Marcus, a wounded soldier who finds consolation and healing in the company of a lovely dragon called Hope. Marcus and Hope embark on a road of recovery and restoration, inspiring others with their strength, courage, and steadfast friendship.

4. A Legacy of Wisdom and Mentorship: Discover the history of Master Dragon Trainer Feng, a famous person whose teachings still inspire and educate young trainers today. Master Feng influenced the lives of numerous trainers and dragons with his wisdom, compassion, and dedication to the art of dragon training, leaving a legacy of greatness and enlightenment.

5. **The Quest for Unity and Cooperation**: Join Captain Elena and her dragon crew on an epic mission to find a legendary treasure that can bring peace and prosperity to their war-torn world. Elena and her crew bring dragons and humans together in a search for unity and cooperation that crosses race and species borders.

6. **The Courage to Dream**: Meet Sarah, a youthful dreamer who defies conventional norms to pursue her passion for dragon training despite obstacles. Sarah overcomes obstacles and prejudice with tenacity, dedication, and an unshakeable belief in herself, becoming one of the most respected trainers in the country, demonstrating that with courage and determination, any ambition is possible.

7. **The Power of Love and Sacrifice**: A touching story about Alex and his dragon friend, Ember, who have a bond of love and sacrifice that transcends space and time. In the face of overwhelming darkness, Alex and Ember's love for each other motivates them to defy fate and rewrite their fates, demonstrating that love knows no bounds and that everything is possible when two people work together.

These inspiring stories of successful dragon trainers remind us of the significant impact that the human-dragon link may have on our lives. May these stories motivate us to pursue our aspirations, conquer difficulty, and enjoy the unique bonds we share with our dragon companions.

LESSONS FROM REAL-LIFE EXPERIENCES

In this section, we'll glean insights and wisdom from dragon trainers' real-life experiences, emphasizing essential lessons learnt via challenges, successes, and the strong bonds built between humans and dragons. These courses include practical advice and philosophical observations on the art of dragon training, as well as the deep bonds formed between trainers and their scaly partners.

1. Real-life experiences emphasize the significance of patience and tenacity during dragon training. Building trust and rapport with dragons requires time and persistent effort, but the benefits of a strong friendship are incalculable.

2. Communication and Understanding: Effective communication and understanding are crucial for successful dragon training. Learning how to listen to your dragon, analyze their cues, and respond correctly builds mutual trust and respect.

3. Adaptability and Flexibility: Training dragons requires adaptability and flexibility due to their unpredictable nature. Being open to new ideas,

strategies, and solutions allows trainers to negotiate obstacles and grab opportunities for advancement.

4. Empathy and Compassion are key to the dragon-human bond. Understanding your dragon's perspective, needs, and emotions develops a stronger tie between trainer and dragon.

5. Resilience and Perseverance: Dragon training involves both accomplishments and losses. Real-life experiences teach us the value of resilience and perseverance in the face of adversity, motivating us to pursue our goals with passion and resolution.

6. Mutual Respect: A solid friendship between trainer and dragon is built on trust and respect. Real-life experiences show that developing trust requires time, consistency, and integrity, yet the relationships formed are unbreakable and long-lasting.

7. Gratitude and Appreciation: Expressing gratitude for the opportunity to work with dragons enhances the training experience and strengthens the bond between trainer and dragon. Real-life experiences remind us to value every moment we spend with our scaly companions and to be grateful for the lessons they teach us.

8. Collaboration and Partnership: Dragon training requires cooperation and partnership between trainers and dragons. Real-life examples demonstrate the importance of cooperation, shared goals, and mutual support in attaining success and conquering obstacles together.

These lessons from real-life situations help us develop a better grasp of the subtleties of dragon training and the tremendous influence it has on the lives of both trainers and dragons. May these ideas motivate and equip trainers to form strong, meaningful ties with their scaly companions, embarking on journeys of growth, discovery, and mutual enrichment.

CHAPTER TEN:

Conclusion:

In the final chapter of our voyage through the realm of dragon training, we consider the lessons learned, the relationships created, and the tremendous influence of the dragon-human alliance. From ancient traditions to modern tales of triumph and transformation, the art of dragon training continues to captivate and inspire our spirits.

Throughout this book, we've looked at the essentials of dragon training, from understanding dragon behavior to fostering trust, forming friendships, and accomplishing incredible things together. We've gone into the rich fabric of dragon lore, discovering the cultural relevance, mythological symbolism, and enduring attraction that dragons evoke in our hearts and minds.

We've traveled with brave trainers and their scaly friends, experiencing their difficulties and successes, pleasures and sorrows, and the deep bonds formed through shared experiences, mutual respect, and steadfast dedication. We've celebrated the triumphs of those who dared to dream, the fortitude of those who persisted in the face of adversity, and the eternal relationships of friendship, love, and devotion that transcend species and time.

As we conclude our investigation of dragon training, let us apply the lessons taught and wisdom gained to our own lives and activities. Let us embrace the values of patience, empathy, and collaboration that are key to the dragon-human partnership, and let us cherish the unique bond between people and dragons with humility, gratitude, and respect.

Whether you are a seasoned trainer or an aspiring enthusiast, may the knowledge and ideas offered in these pages inspire you to undertake on your own journey of discovery, growth, and adventure, accompanied by your scaly friends. May you strengthen the links of trust, understanding, and camaraderie that connect you to your dragons, and may you continue to weave your own stories of bravery, compassion, and triumph into the magnificent tapestry of dragon lore.

As we conclude this chapter of our journey, may we carry the spirit of dragon training with us wherever we go, inspiring others with our stories, improving our lives with our connections, and celebrating the magic and wonder of the dragon-human partnership for generations to come.

With deepest thanks and endless wonder,

[WISDOM .O. WISDOM]

Final Thoughts and Reflections

As we near the end of our voyage through the world of dragon training, it's time to pause and reflect on the profound insights, feelings, and emotions we've had along the way. In this section, we will look at some closing thoughts and observations that capture the heart of our journey and the lessons we've learned along the way.

1. Express thankfulness for our shared adventure. Each chapter, narrative, and lesson has contributed to our understanding of dragon training and strengthened our admiration for the

incredible link between people and dragons.

2. Embracing Growth and Transformation:
Consider how this journey has changed you as a
trainer and individual. Accept the progress,
obstacles faced, and insights acquired,
understanding that each event has helped you
evolve as a dragon trainer and steward of the
natural world.

3. Respecting the Bond Between Trainer and
Dragon:
Pause to recognize the sacred relationship
between trainer and dragon that is at the heart of
our journey. Cherish the moments of connection,
understanding, and camaraderie you share with
your scaly pets, knowing that these ties are
beyond words and will endure a lifetime.

4. Inspiring Others with Your Story: Your
experience as a dragon trainer can encourage
others to pursue their own journeys. Share your
experiences, achievements, and struggles with
others, knowing that your tale has the potential
to instill enthusiasm, interest, and wonder in
those who hear it.

5. Commitment to Lifelong Learning and
Growth: As a dragon trainer, you will embark on
a lifelong path of exploration and learning.
Accept new difficulties, seek out new

knowledge, and be open to the limitless possibilities that await you, knowing that the path of a trainer is one of constant progress and expansion.

6. Commit to fostering a culture of respect, compassion, and conservation in your relationships with dragons and the natural world. Advocate for the protection of dragon species and their habitats, understanding that our actions today will alter the world for future generations of trainers and dragons.

7. Embracing the Magic of the Dragon-Human relationship: This trip has been guided by the dragon-human relationship, which has been magical and wonderful. Let the links formed between trainer and dragon serve as a reminder of the beauty, mystery, and limitless possibilities that await us when we open our hearts to our surroundings.

As we conclude this chapter of our journey, may we carry these final thoughts and reflections with us, knowing that the spirit of dragon training will continue to inspire, uplift, and unite us in our shared pursuit of connection, understanding, and harmony with the dragons that grace our lives.

Encouragement for Aspiring Dragon Trainers

This section is dedicated to individuals who wish to embark on the noble adventure of dragon training. We give words of encouragement, direction, and inspiration to help you along your journey as you take your first steps into the wonderful realm of dragon-human cooperation.

1. Believe in Your Abilities: Believe in your natural capacity to connect with dragons. Trust that you have the patience, empathy, and determination required to form deep and profound friendships with these amazing creatures.

2. Embrace the Journey: Approach dragon training with an open heart and adventurous attitude. Approach each new experience with curiosity, amazement, and a readiness to learn, understanding that every encounter with a dragon offers opportunities for growth and discovery.

3. Seek Knowledge and Guidance: Learn from professional trainers, mentors, and resources to better understand dragon behavior, training strategies, and best practices. Learn from the experience of others who have come before you, and be willing to incorporate fresh ideas and viewpoints into your own training method.

4. Practice Patience and persistence: Develop patience and persistence to overcome hurdles and setbacks during dragon training. Understand that developing trust and rapport with dragons

requires time and regular effort, but the benefits of a solid friendship make the journey worthwhile.

5. Show respect, understanding, and compassion when interacting with dragons. Recognize them as sentient individuals worthy of dignity, autonomy, and comprehension, and go into each training session with a real desire to connect and communicate.

6. Celebrate tiny successes: Celebrate tiny successes as you advance through your training adventure. Whether it's a good training session, a breakthrough in communication, or a moment of connection with your dragon, take the time to recognize and enjoy these milestones as signals of progress and development.

7. Trust in the relationship: Embrace the relationship between trainer and dragon during this shared voyage. Know that your bond with your dragon will provide you with strength, camaraderie, and inspiration as you face life's trials and joys together.

8. Remember Your Purpose: As a dragon trainer, your primary goal is to promote harmony, understanding, and respect between people and dragons. Allow your admiration for these wonderful creatures to guide you as you work to

build a world in which dragons and humans coexist peacefully and mutually appreciate.

To all aspiring dragon trainers, may these words of encouragement kindle the flames of passion and inspiration inside your hearts as you embark on your journey to form meaningful ties with the dragons who inhabit our world. Accept the magic, wonder, and limitless possibilities that await you on this incredible voyage, and may your friendships with your scaly companions bring you joy, fulfillment, and purpose beyond measure.

**********THANKS FOR READING**********